Halogen Cooking Made Simple...

Welcome to Halogen Cooking

CONTENTS

Starters / Appetizers:

PAGE

7 Asparagus and Parma Ham Wraps
9 Avocado Fans with Bacon and Stilton
11 Basic Bread
13 Chicken Liver Pâté with Apricots
15 Curry Wedges
17 French Bread Pizza
19 Garlic and Chilli Prawns
21 Garlic and Chilli Shrimp with Scallops
23 Garlic Mushroom
25 Honey and Mustard Chicken Wings
27 Quesadillas
29 Stuffed Potato Skins

Main Courses / Entrée:

31 Cauliflower Cheese
33 Jerk Chicken
35 Chicken Pie
37 Chilli Con Carne
39 Cod with a Herb Crust
41 Gammon Steak with Honey and Roast Apple
43 L.A. Burgers
45 Leg of Lamb with Rosemary and Garlic
47 Macaroni Cheese
49 Mexican Tuna Steak
51 Monkfish Kebabs with Chilli and Lime Marinade
53 Moroccan Lamb
55 Oriental Salmon
57 Pasta Bake

Main Courses / Entrée: (Continued)
PAGE

59 Pork Chops with Parmesan and Sundried Tomato Stuffing
61 Pork Pittas
63 Posh Fish and Chips Seabass Lemon and Butter
65 Potato and Sausage Breakfast
67 Quick Tandoori Masala Chicken
69 Rack of Lamb with Garlic and Rosemary
71 Ratatouille
73 Roast Beef with Porcini Mushrooms and Red Wine Gravy
75 Roast Chicken with Sage Onion and Cranberry Stuffing
77 Roast Chinese Duck
79 Roast Pork with Peach Stuffing
81 Roasted Vegetables
83 Satay Chicken
85 Seafood Bake
87 Spicy Meat Loaf
89 Stir Fry Chicken with Ginger and Soy Sauce
91 Steak with Thyme Butter
93 Sweet and Sour Cod

Desserts:

95 Baked Pineapple
97 Cheats Crème Brûlée
99 Hot Bananas with Rum and Raisin Sauce
101 Chocolate Indulgence
103 Maple and Pecan Sticky Pudding
105 Oat Flapjack
107 Pear Upside Down Cake

Handy Hint
Instead of mustard use pesto in the cream cheese.

Asparagus and Parma Ham Wraps

Ingredients

16 asparagus tips
4 tbsp cream cheese
2 tbsp mayonnaise
½ tbsp favourite mustard
4 sheets parma ham
½ tbsp chopped fresh parsley
2 tbsp grated gruyère
Pinch salt
Pinch pepper
    Serves 4

Method

1. Get a bowl that the asparagus can fit in and pour over boiling water and leave for five minutes.
2. Mix the cream cheese, mayonnaise, mustard and fresh parsley together and season.
3. Place parma ham on the oven dish and put four pieces of asparagus in each ham slice, then top with the cream cheese mixture. Close the ham and top with gruyère.
4. Grill on high wire rack at 240°C/460°F for 6 minutes or until golden brown. (When using a regular oven place on high grill setting for six minutes until cooked).

Handy Hint
You can use your preferred cheese instead of stilton.

Avocado Fans with Bacon and Stilton

Ingredients

2 ripe avocado
50g 2 oz stilton
3 streaky bacon rashers
Rocket leaves to garnish
Serves 2 / 4

Method

1. Cook chopped bacon under the halogen grill for 5 minutes until crispy on full power 240c / 500.
2. Peel and fan avocadoes and place on oven dish.
3. Place stilton and bacon on top of avocado and cook on high rack at 240°C / 500°F for 5 minutes until cheese is bubbling.
4. Serve with crusty bread and rocket / arugula salad.
(When using a regular grill make sure you pre-heat the grill and follow as per instructions.)

Handy Hint
Add fried garlic or chopped
olives at stage 5 for a different
flavoured bread.

Basic Bread

Ingredients

250g / 9oz plain or bread flour
½ tsp salt
1 tsp sugar
40g / 1½oz melted butter or oil
¼ pt / 160ml warm milk
15g / ½ oz fresh yeast
Flavourings:
Garlic / Olives / Sundried Tomato
            Serves 4

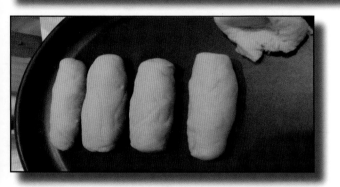

Method

1. Mix the yeast with the milk and sugar, leave for six minutes.
2. Place the flour and salt into a bowl and mix in the melted butter. Add the yeast liquid and mix to a soft dough.
3. Knead the dough for ten minutes until the dough becomes firm and elastified, to save time you can use a food mixer.
4. Place dough into a bowl and cover with a clean damp cloth, and leave in a warm place for ten minutes, the dough will expand.
5. Knead the dough again for two minutes, to reduce it to the original size, you can add any flavorings to your bread now.
6. Decide what shape bread you are going to make and place in the correct cooking dish.
7. Cook in halogen oven on lower rack at 220°C / 440°F for 15 to 25 minutes or until cooked, time will vary on what type and size of the bread you make. (When using a regular oven pre-heat first and follow as per instructions, until cooked.)

Handy Hint
Melt some butter with thyme and pour over the top to preserve the Pâté.

Chicken Liver Pâté with Apricots

Ingredients

250g / ½ lb chicken livers
½ medium finely chopped onion
50g / 2oz butter
8 dried apricot finely chopped
Salt & pepper
1 tbsp mango chutney
¼ tbsp oil
3 tbsp double cream
Serves 5

Method

1. Chop the chicken livers in half, and place onto a round oven tray.
Drizzle with oil, season and mix with the chopped onions.
2. Cook on high rack at 250°C / 500°F for eight minutes on each side then add half the butter and cook for a further one minute or until all cooked.
3. Allow to cool and place in fridge until chilled.
4. Place in a food processor with a mincing blade the cooked chicken livers, mango chutney, the rest of butter, double cream and season again if necessary. Mix until desired consistency then stir in apricots.
5. Place in small ramekin dishes and flatten. Melt a little butter and fresh thyme together then pour over the pâté to seal it. This way it will keep in a fridge for three days. (When using a regular stove, place in a hot frying pan and cook as per method).

13

Handy Hint
Can be served with sour cream
and mayonnaise mixed together
with some chives.

Curry Wedges

Ingredients

2 medium potatoes cut into wedges
1 tbsp curry powder
A pinch garlic salt
1 tbsp sweet chilli sauce
Salt and pepper
3 tbsp olive oil
        Serves 2

Method

1. Place the potato wedges, curry powder, garlic salt, sweet chilli sauce, salt and pepper to taste and olive oil in a large bowl. Mix well.
2. On a round oven tray place the marinated wedges.
3. Place on low tray on full heat at 250°C / 500°F for 25 minutes, stirring occasionally or until cooked.
4. Serve with sour cream and mayo dip, mixed together with some fresh chives. (When using a regular oven pre-heat on high and follow the method.)

15

Handy Hint
Other fillings: Salami, Tuna ,Sweetcorn,
Cooked chicken, Spinach, Cooked mince beef,
Sausage, Bacon, Mozzarella, Ham and pineapple.

French Bread Pizza

Ingredients

1 French stick
3 tbsp tomato purée
Pinch of mixed herbs
6 tbsp tomato sauce
1 onion finely chopped
3 slices/rashers bacon
10 medium mushrooms sliced
2 cups / 8 oz / 220g grated cheddar
1 tsp olive oil
      Serves 4

Method

1. First place the chopped onion, bacon on a tray on the high rack and drizzle with oil. Cook for 8 mins at 240°C / 460°F.
2. While this is cooking, mix the tomato sauce, dried herbs and tomato purée in a bowl.
3. Spead this over the sliced french bread, then top with the cooked onions and bacon. Sprinkle with grated cheese and mushrooms and season.
4. Grill on high rack 240c / 460c for 10 minutes or until golden brown. Serve with rocket / arugula salad and balsamic dressing. (When using a regular grill, place on high heat as per instructions, until cooked.)

17

Handy Hint
Peeled tiger prawns / shrimps can be used instead.

Garlic and Chilli Prawns

Ingredients

180g / 7oz prawns / shrimp
1 tbsp butter, melted
¼ tbsp honey
2 tbsp sweet chilli sauce
2 cloves garlic finely chopped
Salt & pepper
Pinch paprika
1/4 tbsp finely chopped ginger
Juice of half a lime
Serves 2

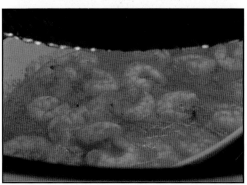

Method

1. Place uncooked peeled prawns into a large bowl.
2. Add butter, honey, sweet chilli sauce, garlic, salt, pepper, paprika, ginger and ¼ of the juice of the lime and mix. Leave to marinate for ten minutes.
3. Place on round oven tray or preferred dish on the top rack of halogen oven on high heat 250°C / 500°F for ten minute each side or until cooked.
4. Finish with the rest of the lime juice and serve with crusty bread and salad. (If using a regular stove, place in a hot frying pan as per method.)

Handy Hint
Great as a main course with stir fry vegetables.

Garlic and Chilli Shrimp with Scallops

Ingredients

250g / 10 oz prawns / shrimps
8 scallops
4 tiger prawns
1 tbsp butter, melted
1 tbsp vegetable oil
2 cloves garlic, finely chopped
Salt and pepper
1 tbsp ginger, finely chopped
Juice from lime
      Serves 4

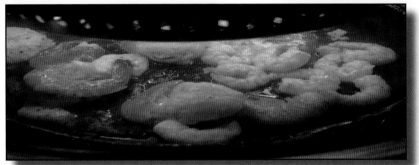

Method

1. Place the uncooked seafood into a large bowl and add butter, garlic, salt, pepper, ginger and ¼ of the juice of one lime and mix, leave to marinate for ten minutes.
2. Place on round oven tray or preferred dish, then on high rack on high heat 240°C / 500°F for ten minutes each side, or until cooked.
3. Finish with a squeeze of lime and salad.
(To cook on a regular stove, place in a hot pan until cooked.)

Handy Hint
Variations in place of Vermouth:
Balsamic vinegar
White wine or Brandy.

Garlic Mushrooms

Ingredients

250g / ½ lb medium sized washed mushrooms
3 cloves finely chopped garlic
75g / 3 oz butter melted slightly
1 tbsp parsley, chopped
Salt and pepper
1 tbsp White Vermouth (optional)
     Serves 2

Method

1. Mix all ingredients together in a bowl, then place on a round tray or prefered oven dish on the high rack in the halogen oven on high heat 235°C / 450°F for twelve minutes stirring half way.
2. Serve with salad and french crusty bread.
(If using a regular oven pre-heat and cook as per method or use a hot frying pan.)

Handy Hint
To make a dip mix 1 tbsp of mayonnaise
1 tbsp of mustard and 1 tbsp of cooked
leftover sauce.

Honey and Mustard Chicken Wings

Ingredients

12 Chicken wings
2 tbsp Dijon mustard
1 tbsp English mustard
2 tbsp Honey
Salt & pepper
1 tbsp lemon juice
1 tbsp brown sugar
Serves 2 / 3

Method

1. Mix the honey, mustards, lemon juice, salt and pepper together and pour over wings. Sprinkle with brown sugar and marinate for ten minutes.
2. Place on the tray within the halogen oven on a high rack and cook on 250°C / 500°F for 20 minutes, turning half way or until cooked.
Serve with salad.
(If using a regular oven pre-heat and cook as per method).

25

Handy Hint
Serve with salsa and sour cream.

Quesadillas

Ingredients

4 flour tortilla wraps
3 tbsp chilli cheese, grated
½ red onion sliced
1 tbsp tomatoes, diced
½ red pepper
100g / 4 oz cooked beef or chicken chopped
Pinch salt
Pinch pepper
        Serves 2

Method

1. Place a flour tortilla wrap on a round oven tray.
2. Add red onion, diced tomatoes, sliced red peppers, cooked chicken and grated chilli cheese.
3. Place in halogen oven on the high rack and cook on high heat 250°C / 500°F for 6 minutes then, add another tortilla wrap and cook for a further 1 minute.
4. Slice into quarters like pizza and serve with salad.
(When using a regular oven, place in the grill on high heat as per instructions, until cooked.)

Handy Hint
Try alternative fillings:
Tuna sweetcorn, Chives,
Ham, Spicy sausage,
Gruyere, Boursin.

Stuffed Potato Skins

Ingredients

2 medium baking potatoes
2 tbsp cream cheese
2 rashers bacon sliced into strips
2 tbsp grated gruyere
Serves 2

Method

1. Cook the baking potatoes on lower rack in the halogen oven on high heat 250°C / 500°F for 45 minutes or until cooked, turning regularly.
2. Once cooked, take out potatoes and place the bacon on a round tray on high heat 250°C / 500°F on the high rack until brown and crisp.
3. While this is cooking, slice the potatoes in two halves, scoop out the inside into a bowl. Add the cream cheese, cooked bacon and season to preference and mix thoroughly. Scoop back into the potato shells, and place on the round tray. Cover in grated gruyere.
4. Place back in the halogen oven on high rack on high heat, 250°C / 500°F until golden brown (if using a regular oven pre-heat and cook as per method).

29

Handy Hint
Sprinkle with paprika.

Cauliflower Cheese

Ingredients

1 Cauliflower part boiled in florets
4 tbsp crème fraîche
250g / 10 oz cream cheese
Pinch mixed dried herbs
5 tbsp cheddar cheese grated
        Serves 4

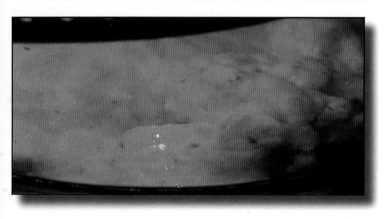

Method

1. Place the cooked cauliflower florets into a round oven dish.
2. Mix the crème fraîche with the cream cheese, mixed dried herbs and 3 tbsp of the grated cheese. Pour over the cauliflower then cover with the rest of the grated cheese.
3. Cook for 10 minutes on high heat 250°C / 500°F until golden brown. (When using a regular oven make sure you pre-heat the oven and follow as per instructions.)

Handy Hint
Use pork fillet instead of chicken
You can also serve with pitta and salad.

Chicken Jerk

Ingredients

1 tbsp jerk seasoning
½ tsp garlic powder
Salt & pepper
1 tbsp mango chutney
1 tbsp sunflower oil
1 tbsp mayonnaise
6 chicken thighs (boned / skinned)
        Serves 3 / 4

Method

1. Place in large bowl the jerk seasoning, garlic powder, salt and pepper, mango chutney, sunflower oil and mayonnaise. Mix thoroughly.
2. Add the chicken thighs and allow to marinate for at least ten minutes in a fridge. (Overnight is even better).
3. Cook in a round oven tray in halogen oven on high rack at 200°C / 400°F for 7 minutes each side or until cooked turning half way.
Serve with rice, kidney beans and salad.
(When using a regular oven pre-heat and follow method).

33

Handy Hint
Add some bacon with
chicken or favourite mushrooms.

Chicken Pie

Ingredients

300g / 11 oz chicken, cubed
1 tbsp cornflour
150ml / ¼ pt milk
150ml / ¼ pt double cream
1 chicken stock cube
1 tbsp fresh parsley
25g / 1 oz butter
Salt and pepper
4 mushrooms
(Pastry)
8 oz plain flour
4 oz butter / lard or half and half
1 tbsp of water
Egg to glaze
　　　　Serves 4

Method

1. To make the pastry, place the plain flour, cold butter and lard with a drop of water into a food processor. Mix using the mincing blade, and turn until the pastry forms a ball. Wrap the pastry in cling film and leave to rest in a fridge for thirty minutes.
2. To make the filling, place the cubed chicken pieces, olive oil, butter and seasoning in a casserole pie dish.
3. Place on the lower rack on high heat 250°C / 500°F for 12 minutes, stirring twice.
4. Add the milk (saving back a little to mix with cornflour), double cream, stock cube and the parsley. Then mix cornflour with the rest of the milk, mix well and add to the filling while stirring well.
5. Cook for a further ten minutes on full heat 250°C / 500°F.
6. While this is cooking roll out the pastry to the size of the dish, then place on top of the filling and glaze with egg and cook until golden brown for 12 minutes on high heat 250°C / 500°F.
Serve with steamed vegtables and boiled new potatoes.

Handy Hint
Great with taco and sour cream.

Chilli Con Carne

Ingredients

1lb / 500g beef, minced / ground
¼ tbsp chilli powder
1 tin kidney beans drained
¼ tbsp cayenne powder
1 tin tomatoes, chopped
2 tbsp tomato puree
4 tbsp tomato ketchup
½ pt / ¼ litre beef stock
1 tbsp plain flour
3 medium fresh tomato quarters
8 mushrooms, washed and sliced
1 onion, finely chopped
2 cloves garlic, chopped
Serves 4

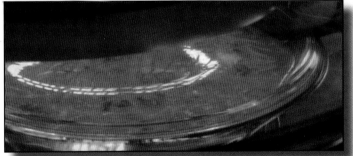

Method

1. In a large oven dish that fits into the halogen oven add the beef, onion and garlic. Cook on the lower rack for 30 mins at 240°C/ 440°F until brown, stirring every 10 mins.
2. Add chilli powder, kidney beans, cayenne powder, tinned tomatoes, tomato puree, tomato ketchup, fresh tomatoes, the mushrooms and mix in the flour. Then add the beef stock and stir in well.
3. Cover with a lid and place in the halogen oven on the lower rack for 1½ hours at 180°C / 350°F, or until cooked, stirring every twenty minutes. Serve with rice.
(when using a regular oven preheat and follow method).

Handy Hint
Serve with new potatoes, carrots, asparagus.

Cod with a Herb Crust

Ingredients

2 medium cod fillets
4 tbsp breadcrumbs
2 tbsp fresh parmesan, grated
1 tbsp fresh parsley, chopped
2 tbsp olive oil
1 tbsp fresh lemon juice
　　　Serves 2

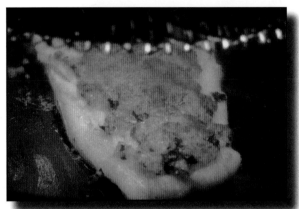

Method

1. Mix the breadcrumbs, cheese and parsley together. Add oil
and lemon juice. Make a paste.
2. Place the cod fillets on a round oven dish, lightly greased with oil
and grease. Place the paste on top of the fish, covering evenly.
3. Place in halogen oven on high grill for twelve minutes at
240°C / 440°F, or until cooked.
(When using a regular oven, place in the grill on high heat as per
instructions, until cooked.)

39

Handy Hint
Serve with new potatoes and vegetables.

Gammon Steak with Honey and Roasted Apple

Ingredients

1 gammon steak
1 apple quartered
1 tbsp honey
   Serves 1

Method

1. Place gammon on a round tray with the apple.
2. Drizzle honey over the gammon and apple.
3. Place on high heat 240°C / 440°F on the high rack for 5 mins each side.
(When using a regular oven, place in the grill on high heat or hot frying pan as per instructions, until cooked.)

41

Handy Hint
Great with cranberry sauce.

L.A. Burgers

Ingredients

500g / 1lb turkey mince
½ tsp ground cinnamon
1 onion finely chopped
1 tbsp fresh coriander /
     cilantro finely chopped
1 egg
1 tbsp / 25g plain flour
Salt & pepper
    Serves 4

Method

1. Place turkey mince into a large bowl and add cinnamon,
onion, coriander / cilantro, egg, flour, salt and pepper and mix and form
into patties.
2. Place on a plate and cover. Rest in a fridge for an hour to help them
set, then cook on the high rack on high heat 250°C / 500°F for 8 mins
each side or until cooked.
3. Serve in a bun or lettuce or with both with pickles and tomatoes and
onions.
(When using a regular oven, place in the grill on high heat or hot frying
pan as per instructions, until cooked).

Handy Hint
In the final stages of roasting
cover lamb joint in mint jelly.

Leg of Lamb with Rosemary and Garlic

Ingredients

Leg of lamb
2 sprigs of rosemary
1 whole garlic, top cut off
5 potatoes
2 sweet potatoes
1 red onion
1 butternut squash
1 tbsp oil
    Serves 4

Method

1. Place the lamb on the low rack, cover with rosemary. Place the garlic on its stalk next to the leg; drizzle all with oil, cook on full heat 240°C / 460°F for ten minutes.
2. Cut the vegetables into chunky pieces (4-5cm), drizzle with oil and season.
3. Add the vegetables to the lamb, turning the lamb over to cook on the otherside for another 10 minutes.
4. Turn again and cook for a further 30 minutes at 180°C / 350°F, turning regularly or cook until how you like it.
(When using a regular oven, pre-heat and follow method.)

45

Handy Hint
You can use pepperoni
instead of bacon and add
fried onions.

Macaroni Cheese

Ingredients

8oz / 200g macaroni
500ml boiling water
1 stock cube
5 oz / 125g cheese, grated
3 tbsp / 75g cream cheese
Salt and pepper
2 rashers bacon, sliced thinly
1 tbsp cornflour
3 tbsp milk
Pinch sugar
Pinch mixed herbs
    Serves 4

Method

1. Put the macaroni pasta in an oven dish, place this on a low rack then pour over with boiling water so the pasta is covered.
2. Add the stock cube and cut up the bacon and cook on full 250c 500f heat for twenty minutes.
3. Stir in the cream cheese and cornflour pre-mixed with a little milk. Stir this in quickly, then add half the grated cheese and season with salt and pepper. Mix in dried herbs and a pinch of sugar.
4. Cook for a further ten minutes, stir and add remaining cheese on top, and cook for another ten minutes on 180°C / 350°F until cheese is golden brown or until cooked.

47

Handy Hint
Serve with bean salad.

Mexican Tuna Steaks

Ingredients

2 raw tuna steaks
2 tbsp Tequila optional
4 spring / green onions, chopped
Juice and zest of one lime
Salt and pepper
Serves 2

Ingredients
(tomato salsa)

3 tomatoes chopped and deseeded
2 spring / green onions
2 tbsp olive oil
Salt and pepper
1 tbsp lime juice
1 Jalapeno pepper, chopped
1 tbsp coriander / cilantro, chopped

Method

1. Place tuna in a bowl and add tequila, spring onions, zest, juice of lime and season. Marinate for ten minutes.
2. Place on a round tray on high grill and full heat 250°C / 500°F, time depends on how you like your tuna, cook accordingly.
Tomato salsa:
1. Place all ingredients into a bowl and serve with the tuna, salad and rice.
(When using a regular oven, place in the grill on high heat or hot frying pan as per instructions, until cooked.)

49

Handy Hint
Use scallops and prawns
instead or with monkfish.

Monkfish Kebabs with Chilli and Lime Marinade

Ingredients

4 metal or wooden pre-soaked skewers
250g / ½lb monkfish, cut into cubes
1 red pepper, cut into 1 inch squares
1 large onion, cut into 1 inch squares
¼ tsp mixed herbs
1 tbsp olive oil
Juice of a whole lime
1 tbsp sweet chilli sauce
   Serves 2

Method

1. Place the cubed monkfish into a bowl and add sweet chilli sauce, mixed herbs, olive oil and half the lime juice.
2. Mix and leave to marinate for ten minutes, then place on skewers with the onion and the red pepper.
3. Place on a grill tray on high rack, high heat 240°C / 440°F for 6 minutes on each side or until cooked.
4. Use the rest of the juice of the lime on the monkish and serve on a bed of rice and salad. (When using a regular oven place in the grill on high heat or hot frying pan as per instructions, until cooked.)

51

Handy Hint
Great in pitta or with cous cous.

Moroccan Lamb

Ingredients

1 tsbp curry powder
2 dried apricots
250g /10 oz lamb steak cubed
½ red onion sliced
100g raisins
1 tbsp pinenuts
sprig coriander to garnish
2 tomatoes deseeded
        Serves 2

Method

1. Place the cubed lamb in a bowl with apricots, onions, curry powder, tomatoes, raisins and pinenuts. Leave to marinate for ten minutes.
2. Place on the high rack at high heat 250°C / 500°F on a baking tray for six minutes on each side or until cooked.
3. Serve with cous cous and coriander.
(When using a regular oven pre heat first and follow as per instructions, until cooked.)

Handy Hint
Add sweet chilli to marinade and
can be served with noodles.

Oriental Salmon

Ingredients

2 salmon fillets
½ tbsp sesame seed oil
1 tbsp hoisin sauce
2 tbsp soy sauce
½ tbsp ginger, peeled, and finely chopped
¼ tbsp garlic, finely chopped
2 Pak Choi, leaves broken off
4 spring / green onions, chopped
      Serves 2

Method

1. Place salmon in a bowl and add the hoisin sauce, soy sauce, ginger, spring / green onion, sesame seed oil and garlic and mix. Leave to marinate for ten minutes.
2. Place the pak choi on the lower rack in the base of the halogen oven and cover up to the rack with boiling water. On the higher rack place the marinated salmon in an oven dish and pour over remaining marinade, cook on 250°C / 500°F (highest temp) for 12 minutes or until cooked how you like it.
Serve on a bed of rice.
 (When using a regular oven, place in the grill on high heat or hot frying pan as per instructions, until cooked).

55

Handy Hint
Pasta can be pre-cooked to save time
so you only need ½ pint / ¼ litre of boiling water.

Pasta Bake

Ingredients
8 oz / 200g pasta shells
1 tbsp olive oil
1 stock cube
1 tin chopped tomatoes in juice
3 tbsp tomato sauce / ketchup
1 medium onion, finely chopped
8 medium mushrooms sliced
2 bacon rasher, sliced thinly
1 tin condensed tomato soup
¼ tsp mixed herbs
3 oz / 75g grated cheese
    Serves 4

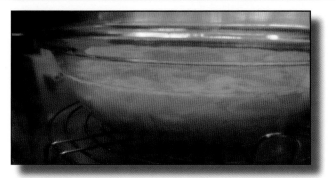

Method

1. Place onion, olive oil and bacon in the oven proof dish that you are going to cook the pasta bake in and place in the halogen oven on low rack, cook on full 250°C / 500°F for 6 minutes.

2. Add pasta to the dish and cover with boiling water, stock cube and mix. Make sure the pasta is submerged and cook for twenty minutes at 250°C / 500°F, stirring twice.

3. Add tomatoes and tomato sauce / ketchup mix. Cook for further 5 minutes at 250°C / 500°F.

4. Add the tin of soup and cover top with cheese. Cook at 180°C / 350°F for 10 minutes or until golden brown .

(When using a regular oven, make sure you pre-heat the oven and follow as per instructions).

Handy Hint
Use basil and pinenuts in place
of sundried tomatoes.

Pork Chops With Parmesan and Sundried Tomato Stuffing

Ingredients

2 pork chops
4 tbsp bread crumbs
1 tbsp fresh parmesan, grated
4 sundried tomatoes, finely chopped
Pinch of mixed herbs
Salt & pepper
2 tbsp of olive oil or oil from the sundried tomatoes
8 new potatoes
Mange tout x 2 servings

Serves 2

Method

1. Start cooking the new potatoes round the edge of the oven for five minutes on 240°C/ 460°F.
2. Combine breadcrumbs, parmesan, salt and pepper, mixed herbs, sundried tomatoes and oil to form a paste.
3. Slice pork chop in two but do not cut all the way, stuff the stuffing mix into the pork chops, and place on the top rack in the halogen oven. Brush with oil and cook on a high temperature 240c/460f for 20 minutes, turning half way.
4. Five minutes before the end of cooking, open the halogen oven, take out the top dish, add one inch of boiling water in the base with the mange tout. Replace the dish and carry on cooking, this way everything will be ready at the same time. (If using a regular oven pre-heat and per method cooking the mange tout separately).

Handy Hint
Great served with
humous and olives.

Pork Pittas

Ingredients

200g / 8oz pork loin
1 tbsp mango chutney
½ finely chopped onion
½ tbsp curry powder
¼ tsp cumin
1 red pepper chopped
Pinch garlic salt
1 tbsp oil
    Serves 2

Method

1. Cut loins into 1cm rounds, flatten into a large circle with a mallett.
2. Mix marinade by combining onion, mango chutney, cumin, curry powder, garlic salt and oil. Add to pork loin and marinate for ten minutes.
3. Cook on a high rack on round oven tray, on for 250°C / 500°F for 6 minutes each side.
4. Serve with red onion and green salad within a pitta bread.
(When using a regular oven place in the grill on high heat or hot frying pan as per instructions, until cooked.)

61

Handy Hint
Add some lemon zest
to the butter.

Posh Fish and Chips

Ingredients
1 sea bass fillet
1 lemon
1 tsp dried dill
1 tsp parsley, chopped
1 potato (cut into chips)
50g butter
Pinch sea salt
        Serves 1

Method

1. Mix parsley with chopped butter and dill.
2. Score the fillet twice and fill with the butter, parsley and dill.
3. Cover potato chips in oil and season.
4. Place chips on a baking tray for 13 minutes on high rack at high heat 250°C / 500°F, turning every 4 minutes.
5. Place fish on same tray and cook for 6 minutes each side or until cooked, not forgetting to turn chips.
6. Serve with slighty grilled skinned cherry tomatoes.
(When using a regular oven, pre-heat first and follow as per instructions, until cooked.)

63

Handy Hint
Once the sausage and potato is cooked mix
up six eggs and pour over and cook to make
a spanish omelette.

Potato and Sausage Breakfast

Ingredients

1 cubed potato
2 tomatoes
½ onion sliced
4 sausages/chorizo
¼ tsp mixed herbs
1 tbsp vegetable oil
2 eggs
Salt and pepper
        Serves 2

Method

1. Put the sausages on a round tray on the high rack and cook at 225°C / 450°F for 3 to 4 minutes each side, until golden brown. Remove and slice.
2. Place onions, potatoes, oil and seasoning in the tray and put back in oven on high, 225°C / 450°F for 25 mins, stirring every 5 minutes.
3. In the last five minutes put the sliced sausages back into the mixture, and put the halved tomato with oil and herbs on the top and place in the centre of the tray.
4. Serve with toast and a fried egg, which can be done in the halogen oven also (cook on a tray on high rack to your taste).
(When using a regular oven, pre-heat and follow as per recipe.)

65

Handy Hint
Serve on a bed of rice
with a tomato and onion
salad and naan bread with
mango chutney

Quick Tandoori Masala Chicken

Ingredients

2 tbsp tandoori masala bbq seasoning
12 chicken fillets
3 tbsp natural yoghurt
¼ tbsp finely chopped fresh ginger
2 garlic cloves crushed
Salt and pepper
1 tbsp sunflower oil
Red onion sliced
¼ tbsp cumin seeds
Juice half lime
        Serves 4

Method

1. Place chicken fillets, tandoori masala, bbq seasoning, natural yoghurt, ginger and garlic in a large bowl. Season with salt and pepper, add oil, onion, cumin seeds and juice of half a lime.
2. Leave to marinate for ten minutes in fridge.
3. Place on round oven tray and place in halogen oven on high rack at full heat 250°C / 500°F for 10 minutes on each side or until cooked.
(When using a regular oven, place in the grill on high heat or hot frying pan as per instructions, until cooked.)

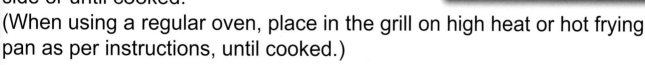

67

Handy Hint
Can be served with mash and steamed vegetables.

Rack of Lamb with Garlic and Rosemary

Ingredients

Rack of lamb
2 sprigs of rosemary
4 cups ready made instant gravy
1 tbsp redcurrant jelly
1 tbsp garlic slivers
Salt & pepper
Serves 4

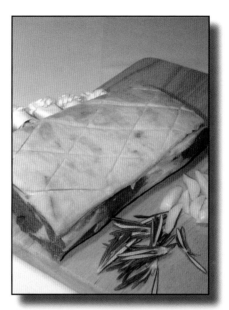

Method

1. Score lamb and use a knife to make small insertions into which add the rosemary and garlic slivers
2. Rub with salt.
3. Place on lower rack on full heat 250°C / 500°F for 30 minutes, turning every 10 minutes.
4. Continue cooking if required to personal taste.
5. Add redcurrant jelly to the hot gravy stir and serve.
(When using a regular oven pre heat first and follow as per instructions, until cooked.)

69

Handy Hint
Great with with grilled / roasted meats and rice.

Ratatouille

Ingredients

1 tin chopped tomatoes	1 yellow pepper large diced
2 tbsp tomato puree	1tbs pine nuts
1 red onion sliced	1tbs olive oil
1 aubergine / eggplant cubed	Salt and pepper
1 courgette / zucchini sliced	½ tbs chopped garlic
1 red pepper large diced	3 tbsp tomato ketchup
Pinch mixed herbs	½ pt / ¼ litre vegetable stock

Serves 4

Method

1. Add the red onion, aubergine, tomato puree, courgette, red pepper, yellow pepper, pinenuts, olive oil, salt and pepper and garlic in an oven proof casserole dish and mix thoroughly.
2. Place in halogen oven on lower rack and cook on high heat 240°C / 440°F stirring every 5 minutes for 20 minutes, so the vegetables are starting to roast as this will really add to the flavour.
3. Add the tin of tomatoes and stir in the ketchup and vegetable stock if necessary to make to the consistency you require.
4. Stir every 5 minutes and cook for a further 20 minutes on temperature 200°C / 390°F.
(If using a regular oven, pre-heat and cook as per method.)

Handy Hint
Works well with rib of beef, also within the gravy, a variety of mushrooms can be used.

Roast Beef with Porcini Mushrooms and Red Wine Gravy

Ingredients

900g / 2lb beef joint
25g / 1oz dried porcini mushrooms
125ml / ¼ pt red wine
1 finely chopped onion
1 heaped tbsp corn flour
1 tbsp butter
¼ tbsp gravy browning
1 beef stock cube
Salt & pepper
            Serves 4

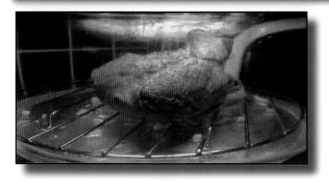

Method

1. Soak the porcini mushrooms in 300ml / ½ pint of hot water and beef stock cube, rub salt on the beef joint.
2. Place chopped onion with wine and porcini mushrooms with the water and stock cube in base of halogen bowl. On the lower rack place the the beef joint and cook for 20 mins at 240°C / 460°F and turn every 10 mins (there are two the other one needs to be taken out also).
3. Then add the butter and gravy browning to the stock in the base of the halogen bowl and mix.
4. Cook for a further 30 mins for medium rare, turning every 10 minutes at 180°C / 350°F. Continue for a further 20 minutes or longer for well done. (When using a regular oven make sure you pre-heat the oven and follow as per instructions).

73

Handy Hint
You can use diced fresh apple instead of cranberry.

Roast Chicken with Sage and Cranberry Stuffing

Ingredients

1 chicken 3 - 4 lb
5 tbsp breadcrumbs
½ onion chopped
2 tbsp cranberry jelly
1 egg
¼ tbsp dried sage
Salt and pepper to taste
½ tbsp oil
Serves 4

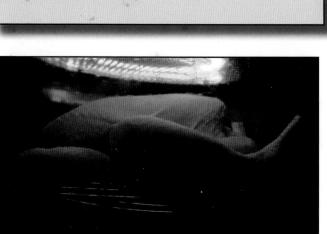

Method

1. Rub chicken skin with salt and pepper, and place on low rack in halogen oven. Cook for 45 minutes turning every 10 minutes at 220°C/ 440°F, then turn it down to 180°C / 360°F for the rest of the cooking time (about another 45 minutes or until cooked).
2. Mix together stuffing ingredients and place in a ramekin dish, place in oven next to chicken for the last 25minutes of cooking.
(When using a regular oven, pre-heat and follow method).

75

Handy Hint
For shredded crispy duck rolls, first boil the duck in water with ¼ tsp Chinese five spice and 1 tbsp soy sauce for 1 hour. Then follow the method from the start, and serve with pancake rolls, cucumber, spring / green onion and plum / hoisin sauce.

Roast Chinese Duck

Ingredients

1 half duck
1 tbsp Chinese five spice
2 bacon rashers
4 tbsp orange marmalade / jelly
or apricot jam / jelly
2 tbsp soy sauce
2 tbsp sesame oil
Salt & pepper
        Serves 2

Method

1. Wrap bacon around the end of the
leg and wing so they don't burn, rub duck with salt and five spice.
2. Cook in the oven for 15 minutes each side on a low rack,
210°C / 405°F.
3. Mix marmalade, five spice, soy sauce, sesame oil and brush over
duck skin. Cook for a further 20 mins, or until cooked to your
satisfaction.
4. Serve with cooked noodles and pak choi.
(When using a regular oven, pre-heat first then follow as per
 instructions)

Handy Hint
Use apple or apricots instead of peaches.

Roast Pork With Peach Stuffing

Ingredients

900g / 2 lb pork chop joint
125 g / 5 oz bread crumbs
¼ tbsp mixed herbs
1 onion finely chopped
1 tin peaches in halves
Salt and pepper
1 onion slice
¼ tbsp mixed herbs
    Serves 4

Method

1. Place the breadcrumbs, ¼ tbsp mixed herbs and onion in a bowl and mix. Add some of the juice from the peaches, chop and add one of the peaches into small pieces and season. Mix into a paste, then make a hole in the centre of your pork joint and stuff with the stuffing, rub the top of the pork joint with salt, place on a roasting tray in the lower rack of the halogen oven.
2. Cook for 1 hour turning every 15 minutes, at 220°C / 440°F. Then cook for another 30 minutes at 180°C / 360°F and put the peaches and the rest of the juice round the pork joint and season again with salt and pepper.
3. Check that the pork joint is cooked all the way through, if not cook at 180°C / 360°F until cooked.
4. Serve with steamed vegetables and roast potatoes.
(When using a regular oven, place in the grill on high heat as per instructions, until cooked.)

79

Handy Hint
Serve with grilled meats.

Roasted Vegetables

Ingredients
1 carrot, peeled, slice diagonally
1 red onion, peeled and cut into 8
1 red pepper, deseeded and sliced
1 butternut squash,
    deseeded and sliced
1 courgette / zucchini sliced
1 sweet potato, sliced
20 cherry tomatoes
¼ tbsp celery salt
¼ tsp garlic puree
Salt and pepper
2 tbsp olive oil
4 sprigs fresh thyme
        Serves 4

Method

1. Place all ingredients into a large a bowl and mix, then place in a round roasting tray.
2. Place in halogen oven on lower rack on high heat
250°C / 500°F stirring about every 5 minutes for 30 minutes.
(When using a regular oven place in the grill on high heat or hot frying pan as per instructions, until cooked).

81

Handy Hint
Serve with crushed peanuts.

Satay Chicken

Ingredients

Juice of ½ lime
8 chicken fillets, sliced
1 tbsp curry powder
2 tbsp peanut butter
1 tbsp mango chutney
1 tbsp mayonnaise
1 tbsp sweet chilli sauce
        Serves 4

Method

1. Place peanut butter into a bowl, place on high rack in halogen oven for 1 minute to soften, then add curry powder, mango chutney, mayonnaise, sweet chilli and lime juice and mix.
2. Mix in chicken fillets strips and allow to marinate for ten minutes.
3. Place on round oven tray on high rack and cook on a high heat 250°C / 500°F for 16 minutes turning half way.
4.Serve on a bed of rice and steamed vegetables.
(When cooking in a regular oven, pre-heat oven first and follow per instructions.)

Handy Hint
You can also add scallops.

Seafood Bake

Ingredients
150g / 6 oz prawns / shrimp, cooked
150g / cod fillet
1 tbsp cornflower
¼ ltr / ½ pt milk
50g / 2 oz butter
50ml double cream
1 chicken stock cube
Pinch of garlic salt
Salt and pepper
2 tbsp fresh parsley, chopped
Crumble mix
100g / 4oz plain flour
50g / 2oz butter
Salt and pepper
2 tbsp parsley, chopped
2 slices of whole grain bread crumbs
75g / 3oz Gruyère cheese, grated
     Serves 4

Method
1. In a casserole dish place cod, milk, garlic salt, stock cube, fresh parsley and butter, place in oven on low rack on high heat 250°C / 500°F for 25 minutes.

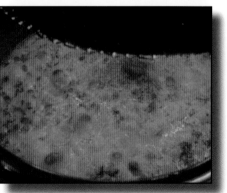

2. With a wooden spoon break the cod up into flakes, mix the cornflower in a cup with a little water till it becomes a liquid, add some of the flavoured milk from the dish then stir the contents of the cup back into the dish.
3. Add prawns and double cream and cook for a further 10 minutes on high heat 250°C / 500°F. While this is cooking, use a food processor with the mincing blade to mix flour, butter, salt, pepper, fresh parsley, whole grain bread, gruyère cheese mix until it looks like breadcrumbs.
4. Then stir filling, add on top crumble mix cook until golden brown on high heat 250°C / 500°F. (When cooking in a regular oven, pre-heat oven first and follow per instructions.)

85

Handy Hint
To make more spicy
add your favourite
chilli sauce.

Spicy Meat Loaf

Ingredients

550g / 1¼ lb minced / ground beef
6 tbsp bread crumbs
1 egg
2 tbsp sour cream / yogurt
2 tbsp tomato ketchup
Mixed dried herbs
1 onion, chopped
Salt & pepper
½ tbsp Worcestershire sauce
    Serves 4

Method

1. Place the beef and breadcrumbs, egg, sour cream, tomato ketchup, mixed dried herbs, onion, Worcestershire sauce, cayenne pepper and salt and pepper into a large mixing bowl and mix well.
2. Place in a large loaf tin and pat down to form a loaf.
3. Cook on the low rack for twenty minutes on 240° / 440°F, then cover with foil and carry on cooking on 190°C / 360°F for 30 minutes or until cooked.
4. Serve with peas, onion rings mashed sweet potatoes.
(When using a regular oven, pre-heat and follow method).

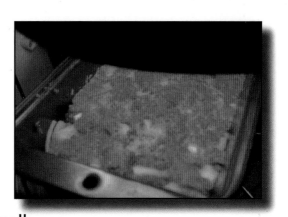

87

Handy Hint
Serve with rice or
tortilla wraps

Stir Fry Chicken with Ginger and Soy Sauce

Ingredients
½ tbsp ginger, finely chopped
2 cloves garlic, finely chopped
3 spring onions, sliced
4 chicken thighs, skinned and deboned
2 tbsp sweet chilli
½ tbsp soy sauce
8 mushrooms sliced in quarters
1 red peppers sliced
1 carrots peel and slice diagonally
Salt pepper
½ tbsp sesame seed oil
     Serves 4

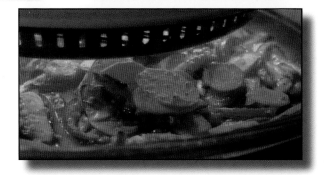

Method
1. Place the ginger, garlic, spring onions, chicken thighs, chilli sauce, soy sauce, mushrooms, peppers, carrots, sesame seed oil, salt and pepper in a large bowl and mix.
2. Allow to marinate for 10 minutes and the flavours will really mix in well. Place all the mixture on a round oven tray on the high shelf in halogen oven, on a high heat 250°C / 500°F for about 10 minutes on each side of the thighs or until fully cooked.
3. Serve on a bed of rice with steamed pak choi, this can be cooked at the same time as the chicken by placing underneath the chicken in a little boiling water.
(Or cook in a wok and follow method).

Handy Hint
Use whole grain mustard
instead of thyme in the butter.

Steak with Thyme Butter

Ingredients

1 steak sirloin
1 tomato cut in half
3 new potatoes
40g / 1 oz butter
Salt and pepper
1 tbsp thyme leaves
1 tbsp of oil
      Serves 1

Method

1. Cut the potatoes into wedges, season and coat with oil, put on a round tray in the bottom of the halogen oven and cook with high heat 250°C / 500°F for 15 minutes.
2. Move the tray of wedges up to the high rack and add the steak, cook for 5 minutes each side or to your taste, then add seasoning.
3. Brush tomatoes with oil, season and place a pinch of mixed herbs on top. Place under grill, and cook for two minutes each side.
4. When cooked, serve with a green salad and top with blended butter and thyme leaves.

Handy Hint
Can use thinly sliced chicken or prawns
instead of cod.

Sweet And Sour Cod

Ingredients

2 skinless cod fillets
2 tbsp tomato sauce
1 tbsp sugar
1 tbsp mango chutney
1 tbsp vinegar
225g pineapple in juice
½ green pepper
½ onion cubed
1 tbsp oil
1 tbsp cornflower
        Serves 2

Method

1. Place cod on round oven tray and season, place in halogen oven on high shelf 240°C / 440°F for 6 minutes turning once.
2. In a bowl add tomato sauce, sugar, mango chutney, vinegar, pineapple, green pepper, onion and cornflower pre-mixed with a little water.
3. Mix well then pour over the cod and cook for a further 10 minutes stirring twice.
4. Serve on a bed of rice.
(When using a regular oven place in the grill on high heat or hot frying pan as per instructions, until cooked.)

Handy Hint
You can use fresh peaches cut
in half, instead of pineapple,
and garnish with fresh basil
leaves.

Baked Pineapple

Ingredients

1 pineapple, quartered
4 tbsp rum
2 tbsp dark brown sugar
      Serves 4

Serve with
Créme Fraîche
or ice cream

Method

1. Score and open pineapple quarters.
2. Mix rum and brown sugar together.
3. Pour over pineapple.
4. Place the pineapple on the high rack at 180°C / 350°F
for 10 minutes

(If using a regular oven pre-heat and cook as per method).

Handy Hint
Can use blueberries or blackberries, or milk chocolate.

Cheats Crème Brûlée

Ingredients

400g / 16 oz custard
or crème brûlée mix
24 raspberries
2 tbsp brown sugar
8 squares white chocolate
    Serves 4

Method

1. In 4 ramekins place the raspberries and two chocolate squares.
2. Mix up the crème brûlée mix or custard and pour into ramekins.
3. Sprinkle the tops with brown sugar.
4. Place on top rack in the halogen oven on a high heat 250°C / 500°F until sugar has caramalized.
As an alternative cooking method, use a blow torch to brown the top of the crème brûlée.

97

Handy Hint
Use brandy instead of rum.
Instead of ice cream used thick cream.

Hot Bananas with Rum and Raisin Sauce

Ingredients

4 bananas
2 tbsp rum
2 tbsp raisins
12 milk chocolate squares
Chocolate sauce
Vanilla ice cream
4 tin foil squares
        Serves 4

Method

1. Place the banana over a square of tin foil, then slice an opening along the banana and fill with chocolate and rasins and sprinkle with rum.
2. Close the tin foil and cook on high 250°C / 500°F for 8 minutes or until hot. Place on plate and serve with ice cream covered with chocolate sauce.

Handy Hint
You can use
white chocolate
instead.

Chocolate Indulgence

Ingredients

100g / 4oz self raising flour
100g / 4oz butter
100g / 4oz caster sugar
3 eggs
100g / 4oz coco powder
100g / 4oz chocolate chips
4 tbsp chocolate sauce
8 chocolate squares
     Serves 4

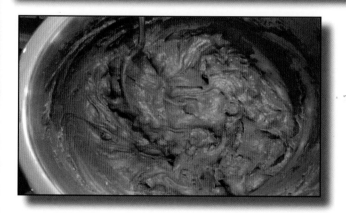

Method

1. Mix the flour, butter, caster sugar, eggs, coco powder and chocolate chips in a large bowl with a wooden spoon or in a food mixer.
2. Butter 4 ramekins and place chocolate sauce and chocolate squares in the bottom, then cover with the cake mix.
3. Place the lower rack in the base of the halogen oven and cover just below the rack with boiling water. Then place the ramekins on the rack and cook on 150°C / 300°F for 40 minutes or until cooked.
4. Serve on a plate with ice cream or thick cream.
(When using a regular oven pre heat first and follow as per instructions, but put a tray with some water in oven to keep the cake moist.)

Handy Hint
Add raisins or sultanas
instead of pecans.

Maple and Pecan Sticky Pudding

Ingredients

6 tbsp maple syrup
12 pecan nuts
125g / 5 oz butter
100g / 4 oz self raising flour
100g / 4 oz brown sugar
2 eggs
4 ramekin dishes
    Serve 4

Method

1. Mix the sugar and butter together then add the egg and flour, stirring and beating all the time until well mixed.
2. Add half the pecan nuts and 2 tbsp of the maple syrup .
3. In the base of the ramekin dishes place the rest of the pecan nuts, maple syrup and butter, then place the cake mix on top.

4. Cover with tin foil, place on the lower rack and cook at 170°C / 340°F for 45 minutes or until cooked. Turn upside down and remove from ramekin to serve. (When using a regular oven, pre-heat first and follow as per instructions, until cooked.)

Handy Hints
Why not try using
dried apricots and cranberries
as an alternative?

Oat Flapjack

Ingredients

225g / 9 oz oats
75g / 3 oz melted butter
50g / 2 oz brown sugar
50g / 2 oz golden or maple syrup
pinch salt
50g / 2 oz dried fruit
     serves 6

Method

1. Butter the baking tray.
2. Mix all ingredients together.
3. Place ingredients into the baking tray on the low rack and cook at 180°C / 360°F for 25 minutes or until cooked. Allow to cool a little and cut into sections.

Handy Hint
Use can use other fruit
instead apricots, peaches, pineapple or apple.

Pear Upside Down Cake

Ingredients

Sponge mix
4 oz / 100g self raising flour
4 oz / 100g butter
2 eggs
4 oz / 100g caster sugar
Base
3 tbsp golden / maple syrup
1 oz / 25g butter
5 glacé cherries
Tinned pear halves, drained
                Serves 4-6

Method

1. Mix sponge, ingredients in a food mixer until creamed together well, or mix with a wooden spoon in a large bowl.
2. Place the golden syrup butter, glacé cherries and tinned pears in the base of a 8" or 20cm cake tin or similar. Place the cake mix on top.
3. Place the tin in the halogen oven on the lower rack, with the higher rack on top with the heat diffuser / steam rack to diffuse the heat. Or if you have not got one of these, place the higher rack on top and cover with a piece of tin foil, punched with holes, just to slow down the cooking process on the top of the cake, cook at 180°C / 360°F.
4. Turn out when cooked upside down on a plate.

INDEX A-Z

A
Asparagus and Parma Ham Wraps 7
Avocado Fans with Bacon and Stilton 9

B
Baked Pineapple 95
Basic Bread 11

C
Cauliflower Cheese 31
Cheats Creme Brulee 97
Chicken Liver Pate With Apricots 13
Chicken Pie 35
Chilli Con Carne 37
Chocolate Indulgence 101
Cod with a Herb Crust 39
Curry Wedges 15

F
French Bread Pizza 17

G
Gammon Steak with Honey & Roast Apple 41
Garlic and Chilli Prawns 19
Garlic and Chilli Shrimp with Scallops 21
Garlic Mushroom 23

H
Honey and Mustard Chicken Wings 25
Hot Bananas With Rum and Raisins Sauce 99

J
Jerk Chicken 33

L
L.A. Burgers 43
Leg of Lamb with Rosemary and Garlic 45

M
Macaroni Cheese 47
Maple and Pecan Cake 103
Mexican Tuna Steak 43
Monkfish 51
Moroccan Lamb 53

O
Oat Flapjack 105
Oriental Salmon 55

P
Pork Chops with Parmesan & Sundried Tomato 59
Pork Pitta 61
Posh Fish and Chips Seabass Lemon and Butter 63
Potato and Sausage Breakfast 65

Q
Quesida 27
Quick Tandoori Masala Chicken 67

R
Rack of Lamb with Garlic and Rosemary 69
Ratatouille 71
Roast Beef with Porcini Mushrooms and Red Wine Gravy 73
Roast Chicken 75
Roast Chinese Duck 77
Roast Pork Peach Stuffing 79
Roast Vegetables 81

S
Satay Chicken 83
Seafood Bake 85
Spicy Meat Loaf 87
Steak with Thyme Butter 91
Stir Fry Chicken With Ginger and Soy Sauce 89
Stuffed Potato Skins 29
Sweet and Sour Cod Pasta Bake 93
U
Upside Down Cake 107

If you have any questions regarding the recipes within this book, please feel free to write to us at:

cook@paulbrodel.co.uk

Why we love Halogen Oven Cooking

In times gone by many years ago, before electricity in the home, kitchens always had a big oven heated by fire, but you also had the big open fires with the roasting spit-handcrank (rotisseie) in front for such things as roasting lamb, suckling pig and roasting chickens, as well as other birds.
The reason for this was radient heat energy. Its intense heat sealed the meat on the outside making it suculent and juicy on the inside. This helped to render down the fat, so the meat was not sitting in it. This makes it better for you than in an oven where it is required for extra fat to be added to the baking tray, to stop the meat from drying out and often sitting in the fat.

Top tips for your halogen oven

1) When steaming vegtables always use boiling water in the base of your oven to save time on heating up. Place the boiling water in first before turning the cooker on. I tend to put vegetables on the low rack and put the high rack on top with the round oven tray and fill with boiling water which will generate the steam when the halogen heat hit the water, the fan above then moves the steam round the cooker. I steam at 140 c 280 f.

2) When grilling such things as bacon you can put tin foil in the base to make it easier to clean after.

3) As a rough rule when cooking meat joints on the low rack, I tend to start on a high heat to seal the meat. This keeps the juices in. Then lower to the tempurature required. When cooking things that you want well done, I use the extender ring to make the cooking process more gental. This will cook the meat more evenly. I also tend to turn joints during cooking.

4) When cooking casseroles, always use an oven dish that fits in the halogen bowl so air can circulate round. In this dish, fry off the meat first with the vegtables. Then I add the liquid and cover with foil wrap. I have also used oven proof glass lids to keep the liquid in and stop it from drying out. Then I turn down the tempurature as I would in a regular oven.

All temperatures given are a rough guide, always check the food has been throughly cooked before consumption.